T0165603

The
Seven
Commandments of
Foolishness

Godman Akinlabi

WESTBOW·
PRESS
A DIVISION OF THOMAS NELSON
& ZONDERVAN

Note: Unless otherwise stated, all Scriptures are from NKJV.

Photo credit to Limelights Portraits, Beechwood, Priorsfield Rd Godalming
Surrey. GU7 2RG 01483 449442 www.limelightportraits.co.uk

WestBow Press books may be ordered through
booksellers or by contacting:

WestBow Press
A Division of Thomas Nelson & Zondervan
1663 Liberty Drive
Bloomington, IN 47403
www.westbowpress.com
1 (866) 928-1240

ISBN: 978-1-4908-1502-2 (sc)
ISBN: 978-1-4908-1503-9 (e)

Library of Congress Control Number: 2013920361

Printed in the United States of America.

WestBow Press rev. date: 11/27/2013

Acknowledgements

This book started out as a message series of the same title, which I shared with The Elevation Church in 2011. On completion of the series, several members of the congregation urged me to develop a written adaptation that would preserve its principles for posterity. I am thankful for the encouragement of this wonderful, teachable congregation and its leaders, who have supported me and have given me time to grow in resourceful thinking. I am truly blessed and privileged to be your pastor.

I am very grateful to Timothy Aderemi, Tunde Usidame, Tunji Iyiola, Segun Iselaye and Bode Adesina for the parts they played in putting this book together. My special thanks goes to my very talented editor, Chinny Ugoji, for her great work on the book as well as for granting me the permission to use her original story, 'The Ostrich and The Eagle.'

Many thanks to my siblings, friends, mentors and teachers; particularly my spiritual parents, Pastors Sam and Nike Adeyemi, whose instructions have enriched my life. A special appreciation also goes to Philip Baker, whose book: 'Wisdom:

The Forgotten Factor of Success', inspired this teaching on foolishness.

To my precious wife, Bolarinwa and my two beautiful girls, Oluwajomiloju and Oluwayojusimi- growing with you has compelled me to increase in wisdom. I love you all.

To God, the source of true wisdom, this is all about you.

Contents

It is easier for the wise to learn from the foolish
than for the foolish to learn from the wise.

—Zig Ziglar

Introduction

Like many Blackberry users, I appreciate smart, humorous display pictures, and I have been known to use some of these interesting images on occasion. One such picture was a cartooned image of an awe-inspiring Moses who had just received the Ten Commandments on Mount Sinai. The twist? He reverently bore in each hand two iPads instead of two tablets of stone. I thought it was a smart way for Christianity and technology to share a good laugh.

I also realized that practically everybody got the joke. It didn't matter if we were Christian, Muslim, Hindu, or atheist; somehow we all heard the phrase "the Ten Commandments." As a matter of fact, I am yet to see a dictionary that defines the word *commandment* without some reference to Moses' receipt of God's holy law for the children of Israel.

A commandment is a mandate, a charge, or an order that usually emanates from a divine ruler. The force of the word *commandment* conveys that the instructions are absolute and do not allow argument, disobedience, or negotiation. Very few words in the English language carry such unequivocal power, and as a result, it is not a word that is wielded lightly or carelessly. With this understanding I have written *The Seven Commandments of Foolishness.*

Nobody wants to be thought of as a fool; yet daily we identify actions or repercussions that can only be the results of foolish acts and thoughts. With literally hundreds of thousands of books written about acquiring wisdom, good judgment, and common sense, the big question remains: Why are many people still trapped in a web of continual folly? Could it be that wisdom is more elusive than we think, or is it simply the exclusive preserve of a few? As I pondered this, I reasoned, "If true darkness is just the absence of light, does it not follow that wisdom is simply the absence of folly?" My hypothesis is that perhaps if people know what acts amount to foolishness, they can eliminate them from their lives and, almost by default, enter into an era of wisdom.

I hope this book serves as a mirror for the "fool" as well as an instruction manual for the "righteous." May the foolish recognize and repent from his or her folly and may the wise person increase in learning. It is my prayer that all who read this book will, by the power of the Holy Spirit, break *all* seven commandments of foolishness and go on to display the wisdom and the excellence of God.

Godman Akinlabi.

The First Commandment

Thou Shall Not Think

The Ten Bridesmaids

Then the Kingdom of Heaven will be like ten bridesmaids who took their lamps and went to meet the bridegroom. Five of them were foolish, and five were wise. The five who were foolish didn't take enough olive oil for their lamps, but the other five were wise enough to take along extra oil. When the bridegroom was delayed, they all became drowsy and fell asleep.

At midnight they were roused by the shout, "Look, the bridegroom is coming! Come out and meet him!"

All the bridesmaids got up and prepared their lamps. Then the five foolish ones asked the others, "Please give us some of your oil because our lamps are going out." But the others replied, "We don't have enough for all of us. Go to a shop and buy some for yourselves."

But while they were gone to buy oil, the bridegroom came. Then those who were ready went in with him to the marriage feast, and the door was locked. Later, when the other five bridesmaids returned, they stood outside, calling, "Lord! Lord! Open the door for us!"

But he called back, "Believe me, I don't know you!" (Matthew 25:1–12 NLT)

> Don't act thoughtlessly, but understand
> what the Lord wants you to do.
> —Ephesians 5:17 NLT

Many people in our world today live unproductive lives because their thinking faculties are *grossly* underutilized. Unfortunately, it's been discovered that a good proportion of this nonthinking populace professes to be committed, Bible-wielding Christians. It appears that while learning to trust God and cast all cares upon Him, Christians have erroneously cast all their reasoning and intelligence upon Him too. God is not responsible for our minds or the way they work; we are. God expects us to demonstrate wisdom, knowledge, and understanding through biblical, Spirit-led thought processes.

However, many Christians constantly walk around in a cloudy, vacant state of mind, not knowing who they are, where they are coming from, or where they are going. They just expect God to wake them daily with wondrous miracles for them to enjoy. Ephesians 3:20 says, "God is able to do exceedingly, abundantly far above all we could ever *ask* or *think*" (emphasis added). Miracles don't occur in a vacuum; you have to actively *think* and *ask* God for direction and provision. Proverbs 23:7 states, "For as he thinks in his heart, so is he." In other words, a person's life and character is the summation of his or her thoughts. Everything you are today is a direct result of how much thought you have put into all your activities.

I once heard someone say that to be unwise, you must cease from all productive mental activity. The easiest way to be foolish is to shut your mind to learning and to maintain your status quo. A person who stops learning, stops growing. And once you stop growing, you start dying. Conversely, to be wise, you must open your mind to challenging thoughts, ideas, and possibilities. The human mind is like a parachute—it only works when it's open. Whereas jumping with an open parachute can be an exciting, exhilarating experience, jumping with a closed parachute results in certain death. An open parachute gives you wings; a closed parachute gives you a face full of pavement.

Aren't We Always Thinking?

Since a living brain always registers some sort of activity, it may seem false to say that people don't think. However, *thinking* here doesn't refer to just brain activity, but rather to a *deliberate* exercise where a person exercises his or her mind to ponder, reflect, calculate, ruminate, muse, brood over, brainstorm, or analyze a particular subject matter. This kind of thinking has brought breakthroughs in science, arts, and technology.

Imagine if we were to expend the same effort thinking about the omniscient Word of God? The Bible calls this kind of deep thinking *meditation*. As we meditate, God communicates to us through our minds and reveals ideas and secrets that sink into our spirits. When these ideas and secrets are applied, they bring wondrous results. The insight derived from meditation is what separates the fool from the wise. Psalm 1:2–3 describes the results of meditation for those who choose to engage in biblical meditation.

His delight is in the Law of the Lord and in His Law does he meditate day and night. He shall be like a tree planted by the rivers of water, that brings forth its fruit in its season, whose leaf shall not wither; and whatsoever he does shall prosper.

Deep thinking, or meditation, requires discipline and commitment. A lot of times, the challenge isn't that people don't want to think; rather, they just don't want to put in the effort deep thinking requires. As a result, many people allow distractions to take over their minds and do their thinking for them. I describe these distractions as "thought deterrents."

Here are some common thought deterrents:

- **Technology:** Thanks to the Internet, round-the-clock television, smartphones and video games, shiny, inanimate gizmos have lured many minds away from productive thinking. Even "harmless" cartoons can be thought deterrents, and parents must ensure that their children don't stay glued to the TV for hours. The irony is that TV addicts watch the product of other people's deep thoughts. Where is the product of your own thought, and who is celebrating it?

- **Functions:** Have you noticed that there's always something happening in your vicinity? It could be a wedding, a concert, or a sporting event. Whatever it is, your days and nights are fully occupied by social activities. While there's nothing wrong with being social, nurturing a "party spirit" that constantly keeps you from engaging in productive reasoning will keep you in a state of foolishness.

- **Fruitless discussions:** Engaging in debates about sports, politics, current affairs, and even religion do not equate to deep thinking. These discussions are rarely an exchange of productive ideas but are usually forums for prideful displays of unapplied knowledge and opportunities to make disparaging remarks. Many people gather to spend hours verbally tearing down the government, their bosses, or their neighbors and achieve absolutely nothing.

- **Addictions:** Alcoholism, drug addiction, sex addiction, pornography, gluttony, and the like all result in an addict being in a constant state of thoughtlessness. An addict always obeys this first law of foolishness. I have yet to see a drunk who inspires wisdom in his or her listeners or a sex addict who doesn't destroy his or her own life by surrendering to the spirit of lust.

- **Miscellaneous attractions:** From going to the mall and window shopping to reading magazines and novels ... these activities, though not bad in themselves, can become time wasters and thought deterrents when they are practiced too often. You must learn to do all things in moderation and apportion the most time to do the things that are really expedient.

Newton's law of motion states that "an object will remain in a position of rest until a relevant force is applied." I believe this law also applies to life's issues. An unfavorable situation will remain the same until a mental force is applied. It takes mental exertion to create beauty—be it in a career, business relationships, marriage, or other endeavor. Nothing becomes beautiful automatically. Creativity starts in the mind; by engaging in productive mental activity—in other words, thinking and ruminating—we create the force or idea that will move things from a thought to reality.

Too Little Too Late?

At certain stages in our lives, nature forces us to think. It could be right after graduation when the job market stares you squarely in the face; it could be at the marriage altar, when you realize you are about to join yourself to another human being for life; it could be at the moment your wife announces she is pregnant and you realize the cost of training a child from kindergarten to university. In any case, suddenly you are thinking—but you are thinking panic-stricken thoughts about how success in this new phase of life might be nothing but a dream. Living a thoughtless life leaves your think tank empty when you need a breakthrough idea.

While you are definitely better off strategizing and preparing for your future long before a crisis point, it is never too late to seek God's help. Hebrews 4:16 says, "Let us therefore come boldly to the throne of grace, that we may obtain mercy and find grace to help in time of need." At this point, turn to God in prayer and study the Word fervently. God in His mercy promises that He will make a way of escape, but you have to stay fervent in prayer and study. In His Word you will find the blueprint for a successful life.

Most products come with a manufacturer's manual that explains what the product is and how it works. Some people read the manual before assembling the product, while others dive into the product and try to figure it out how to use it as they go along. The latter group hardly ever utilizes the product to its full potential, because they are simply unaware of all it can do. If we would only take the time to inquire in His Word and prayer, we would save time and experience a lot less pain than we would while living by trial and error. Refusing to pray and study the Bible is a sure way to obey the first commandment of foolishness.

Thou Shall Think

The only way to break the first commandment of foolishness is to *think*. Here are three tips on how to engage your mind in productive thinking.

- **Think intentionally:** Be deliberate about your decision to think deep thoughts. First identify the problem and then ponder how to solve it. Ask yourself, "How do I resolve this issue? What is the best course of action to conquer it?" Stay results oriented. Many people engage in deep thoughts without knowing it. For instance, in a city like Lagos, Nigeria, because of the usual hectic traffic situations, it is normal to be very deliberate about your route choices when setting out to any destination. This often means mapping out the best possible route to avoid the worst of the traffic. In the same way, dissect a challenge by thinking deeply. Examine it bit by bit. Perhaps you are an unemployed graduate. Rather than wonder and weep about why no one will hire you, ask yourself, "How can I earn a living? What are my skills and talents? How do I convert them into a livelihood?" Just as you try to map out a path to reach your destination in spite of traffic, you can prayerfully engage in strategic thoughts to map out your career path and future.
- **Ask the Holy Spirit for help:** Allow me to use the traffic example again: Sometimes as I drive, I get to a

critical intersection, and I know that in spite of all my careful planning, I can't predict the traffic in the roads up ahead. At that point, I ask the Holy Spirit for His direction, because He knows the best route for me to take. Now you might be rolling your eyes thinking that hearing such a specific answer from the Holy Spirit is easier said than done, but the truth is that I can discern when the Holy Spirit speaks to me because I spend time in deep thought and communication with Him. Since I am used to Him directing my thoughts and giving me ideas when I pray and meditate, I can tell when He urges me to go to the left or to the right. If you commit to opening the lines of communication through prayer and meditation (deep thoughts), you can ask the Holy Spirit for help and guidance when you are at the crossroads of life.

- **Be focused:** Perhaps you are agonizing over where to send your children for their schooling. Choosing a school is a very important decision for most parents, as this choice will influence your child for the rest of his or her life. If the burden of this important decision has you in a state of panic, be calm and *persistent* in prayer. If you catch your mind roaming being overrun with worry, rein it in and engage it in Scripture. For instance, 2 Corinthians 1:20 says, "And you have an anointing from the Holy one and you know all things." Quell those doubts by reminding yourself that you are anointed and you have the ability to know God's mind concerning the best school for your children. Pray in the Spirit while keeping those Scriptures in mind and keep yourself from distractions.

To further help your focus, you may even create a specific physical space where you think. You may place Scriptures or pictures on the wall in this space that will keep those productive thoughts before your eyes. If it is about your business, consider putting a chart or project timeline on the wall. Seeing these things in your special place will keep your mind focused on the issues at hand.

You often hear, "the best way to keep a secret from a fool is to put it in a book". These days, it is increasingly common to find people who would rather watch a film adaptation of a book rather than read the book on which the movie was based. It is also considered more fun to pay to see a game or a concert than visit a free museum. *We must stop swapping wisdom for pleasure.*

There is nothing wrong with going to movies, concerts, or games, but they must not be your priorities. Purposely align your actions in a manner that reflects your thirst for knowledge. Don't swap church for golf. When reading the paper, don't skip the finance segment and make a beeline for the comics. Spend more time reading materials that engage your mind in positive, constructive thoughts and less time on gossip magazines. A constant diet of tabloids, fashion, and comics may entertain you, but it will ultimately distract your mind from productive thoughts that engender change.

Engaging in deep thinking is a habit-forming activity. The more you engage in it, the more it will become as natural as brushing your teeth. Most importantly, opening the parachute of your mind will move you one step further away from a life of foolishness.

The Second Commandment

If It Feels Good, Do It!

The Seductress

As I stood at the window of my house
looking out through the shutters,
Watching the mindless crowd stroll by,
I spotted a young man without any sense
Arriving at the corner of the street where she lived,
then turning up the path to her house.
It was dusk, the evening coming on,
the darkness thickening into night.
Just then, a woman met him—
she'd been lying in wait for him, dressed to seduce him.
Brazen and brash she was,
restless and roaming, never at home,
Walking the streets, loitering in the mall,
hanging out at every corner in town.

She threw her arms around him and kissed him,
boldly took his arm and said,
"I've got all the makings for a feast—
today I made my offerings, my vows are all paid,
So now I've come to find you,
hoping to catch sight of your face—and here you are!
I've spread fresh, clean sheets on my bed,

colorful imported linens.
My bed is aromatic with spices
and exotic fragrances.
Come, let's make love all night,
spend the night in ecstatic lovemaking!
My husband's not home; he's away on business,
and he won't be back for a month."

Soon she has him eating out of her hand,
bewitched by her honeyed speech.
Before you know it, he's trotting behind her,
like a calf led to the butcher shop,
Like a stag lured into ambush
and then shot with an arrow,
Like a bird flying into a net
not knowing that its flying life is over.

So, friends, listen to me,
take these words of mine most seriously.
Don't fool around with a woman like that;
don't even stroll through her neighborhood.
Countless victims come under her spell;
she's the death of many a poor man.
She runs a halfway house to hell,
fits you out with a shroud and a coffin. (Proverbs 7:6–27 *The Message*)

To stay within the confines of foolishness, you must base all your decisions on the emotions of the moment. This is the crux of the second commandment. Therefore, if you feel the urge to slap someone, even if it happens to be the president of your country, just do it. Why? Because at the moment your palm is itchy, and all it feels like doing is slap.

Sounds stupid, doesn't it? It certainly is, but from time to time, we all obey this second commandment. This is why, in spite of a person's acquiescence during premarital counseling never to lift his hand against his wife in violence, just months after he has said his vows, the same man suddenly finds himself promising to beat his wife into submission. If the woman in question doesn't conform to his wishes, this man will make good on his promise of corporal punishment and thereafter blame it on heightened emotions. Most men feel remorse and some shame after physically abusing their wife, and to excuse their behavior they often blame it on the Devil. The truth is that they acted on the emotions of the moment; blaming it on demon possession is just a convenient way to excuse foolishness. It *felt* good to be physically stronger and it *felt* even better to unleash that power on their wife.

The women aren't off the hook either. The average woman's verbal skills are far more advanced than a man's, so even though she may be unable to hurt him physically, she can attack with words. When such a woman is asked why and how she could say something so cruel to a man she supposedly loves, she too relies on the usual defense of demon possession or emotional provocation. She says she just couldn't help herself. That isn't true either. It *felt* good to wound her husband with cruel words that she knew would pierce his heart and cause severe damage to his ego. It *felt* good to see the effect of the lethal barbs she flung her husband's way. Acting on those feelings, whether you are a husband or a wife, can cost you your marriage, your children, and your future.

If we live only for what feels good or gratifying, we will ruin our lives and possibly the lives of our loved ones. For instance, in Genesis 34, Simeon and Levi, embittered by the rape of their sister Dinah, pretended to forgive Shechem (her rapist) and then murdered every single man in his town. Though they felt justified and their anger was assuaged after the bloodshed, they and their descendants received a curse instead of a blessing at their father's, Jacob's, deathbed. Acting on emotions can cost you not only your present but also your future.

Emotions are unreliable because they are unstable by nature. In fact, some people's feelings are as varied as the weather. If it's sunny, they're happy, if it's rainy, they are not. Imagine having such an erratic person for a spouse? One minute he is as jolly as can be and the next minute his face is like a thundercloud. You ask, "Did I do anything wrong?" And all he says is, "I don't want to talk." How do you build a stable, happy home with such a person?

"I Really Can't Control Myself"

Some people claim that they simply cannot control their emotions. False. Everyone consciously or unconsciously makes decisions based on an analysis of cause and effect. On a Monday morning, many people don't *feel* like going to work, but they do. This is because they know that if they treat their jobs lightly, they could quickly become unemployed. As for being unable to control ones temper, have you ever seen a so-called hot-tempered person stop in mid-tirade to take an important phone call? One minute he is shouting at the top of his lungs and the next minute he is chatting pleasantly and politely with that important person. You see, you can control your emotions when you know your actions can affect you negatively or positively. Interestingly, after the phone call, he can pick up his rant from where he stopped. It means temper *is* controllable, but he only controls it when it benefits him. Blaming wrong actions on an inability to control yourself is not only self-centered but also self-deceit. It is a classic case of foolishness.

Some people believe that the attitude you choose is hinged on your freedom of expression. "After all, not everybody has to be Mr. Nice Guy. Therefore if I *feel* like sleeping with somebody's fiancé or *feel* like having premarital sex, that's fine. If I *feel* like dishonoring my parents, that's my prerogative. If I *feel* like tormenting weaker or handicapped people, that's just their luck." That's foolishness speaking. True freedom doesn't lie in the ability to do what feels good but rather in the ability to do what is right. Please understand: *a person who is controlled by his or her emotions is a slave.* He or she is at the mercy of whatever whim the flesh conjures in his or her mind.

The appeal of living solely by how one feels is the possibility of living a life that exempts you from practicing endurance. Endurance is the ability to suffer something painful or uncomfortable patiently. It is not a pleasant experience but rarely do we achieve anything of lasting value without withstanding some tough times. The refusal to endure is the main reason divorce rates have skyrocketed. People no longer see the need to endure the necessary trials of marriage. They get married because it feels good and get divorced when the feeling passes. Today people have done away with the marriage institution and simply cohabit as "partners." Once the arrangement no longer suits them, they move on. Those who still enter into marriage adopt prenuptial agreements in anticipation of a divorce, which usually occurs. People don't understand that there is genuine freedom in committing to share your life with someone, with the knowledge that no matter what winds may blow, you have a partner for life.

When the question of sexual purity comes into play, people always ask, "If sex is bad, why did God create it? And if it's good, why does it have conditions?" God said sex is a good *within* the provisions of marriage. True sexual freedom can be experienced only in marriage, where you don't have to perform like a sex slave or use sex as a bribe for love. You are able to love your spouse—spirit, soul, and body—with no strings attached. That is real freedom.

Delayed Gratification and the "Inconvenience" of Endurance

The average human being hates to endure. However, endurance is a kingdom principle. God has designed life so that to reap a reward, we often have to endure a season of toil, discomfort, or even hardship. Our Lord Jesus set the ultimate example for us when He came to earth to save us. "For the joy that was set before Him, He endured the cross and despised the shame" (Hebrews 12:2). It didn't feel good for Him to die, but because He endured for our sakes, we became free from sin forevermore!

In the same vein, 2 Timothy 2:3 says, "You therefore must endure hardship as a good soldier of Christ." Most of us will never have to endure the kind of hardship the apostles endured, such as imprisonment, stoning, beatings, starvation, and all manners of persecution. Yet in the face of such hardship, they endured and have become our cloud of witnesses. Exercise restraint, appreciate the purpose of the delay, and endure the momentary discomfort. The rewards will definitely be gratifying.

Emotional Freedom: Just Say No

If you have been a slave to your emotions, it's time to be set free. You may be a shopaholic, but rather than spend money because it feels good, look at that credit card and just say no. I mean it; say it out loud. I once read a story about a boy who stole his father's credit card. His friend asked him, "Has your father reported the stolen card to the authorities?" The boy replied, "No, Dad said the thieves are ringing up fewer charges on the card than my mother did." A shopaholic is simply a person who has not trained himself or herself to say no. Set yourself free from that oppressive spirit.

Say no to extra marital affairs. Say no to abuse or crime. Say no to greed. Say no to laziness. Say no to unproductive living. Say no to violence and bouts of anger. Say no to sin. Like a good soldier of Christ, endure the discomfort of the moment and reap the joy of the future.

Say this out loud, "I am not a feeling. I am a spirit. Feelings may change, but truth remains the same. The Word of God is the same forever! I am not moved by what I feel. I am and will forever be moved only by the Word of God! Hallelujah."

The Third Commandment

Thou Shall Never Be Serious

The Boy Who Cried Wolf

There once was a shepherd boy who was bored as he sat on the hillside watching the village sheep. To amuse himself he took a great breath and sang out, "Wolf! Wolf! The wolf is chasing the sheep!"

The villagers came running up the hill to help the boy drive the wolf away. But when they arrived at the top of the hill, they found no wolf. The boy laughed at the sight of their angry faces.

"Don't cry 'wolf,' shepherd boy, when there's no wolf!" said the villagers. They went grumbling back down the hill.

Later the boy sang out again, "Wolf! Wolf! The wolf is chasing the sheep!" To his naughty delight, he watched the villagers run up the hill to help him drive the wolf away. When the villagers saw no wolf, they sternly said, "Save your frightened song for when there is really something wrong! Don't cry 'wolf' when there is no wolf! "But the boy just grinned and watched them go grumbling down the hill once more.

Later he saw a real wolf prowling about his flock. Alarmed, he leaped to his feet and sang out as loudly as he could, "Wolf! Wolf!"

But the villagers thought he was trying to fool them again, and so they didn't come. At sunset, everyone wondered why the shepherd boy hadn't returned to the village with their sheep. They went up the hill to find the boy. They found him weeping.

"There really was a wolf here! The flock has scattered! I cried out, 'Wolf!' Why didn't you come?"

An old man tried to comfort the boy as they walked back to the village. "We'll help you look for the lost sheep in the morning," he said, putting his arm around the youth. "Nobody believes a liar ... even when he is telling the truth."

To be serious means to act in a thoughtful, careful, profound, and solemn manner. To be unserious is to be lighthearted and to deliberately avoid the influence of wisdom. In the present-day social scene, the above definitions seem to imply that a serious person is a stick-in-the-mud while an unserious person is the life of the party. Don't be quick to jump to that conclusion. Let's have a look at what the Word of God says.

> Go to the ant you sluggard! Consider her ways and be wise, which having no captain, overseer or ruler, provides her supplies in the summer, and gathers her food in the harvest. How long will you slumber, o sluggard? When will you rise from your sleep? A little sleep, a little slumber, a little folding of the hands to sleep- so shall your poverty come on you like a prowler, and your need like an armed man. (Proverbs 6:6–11)

While in my office one day, I had a drink and placed my glass, which still contained a small amount of juice on my table. Not long afterward, I noticed a couple of ants around the glass. How did they know so quickly that there was some provision in the vicinity? That's the amazing thing about ants: even if you keep the sugar in a locked safe, they will find a way to get into it. As small as they are, they utilize every ounce of grace, skill, and capability God placed in them to sustain their lives. The only way to keep sugar safe from ants is to store it in an airtight container that hinders their senses and abilities.

Ants are tenacious and diligent, yet a child can snuff out their lives with his or her small finger. Human beings, on the other hand, are giants with a cranial capacity of about 550 cubic inches (1,400 cubic centimeters), yet we don't think or plan half as much as a mere ant. Rather, we avoid wisdom and make light of life, thinking, "let's eat, drink and be merry, for tomorrow we die" (1 Corinthians 15:32). If an ant, whose life can be so easily extinguished, insists on living in wisdom and foresight, why not you?

A lack of seriousness is a critical spiritual illness. In the Elevation Church, we close each service by speaking the words of Psalm 1:1-3. Psalm 1:1 says, "Blessed is the man, who walks not in the counsel of the ungodly, nor stands in the path of sinners, nor sits in the seat of the scornful." We remind ourselves that there is a blessing (an empowerment to prosper) when we refuse to treat life with disdain or regard it as a joke. Have you ever met a person who always has one wisecrack or another, who never has a word of wisdom to share? Such a person may be good for a laugh but he or she will never be invited to deliberate when life-changing issues are being discussed. We were created to be kings and priests, not court jesters.

Don't misunderstand; there is nothing wrong with having a laugh or being of good cheer. As a matter of fact, the Christian should live a life full of joy. It is good to make merry and to be happy, but remember that there is a time and a season for everything. There is a time to laugh out loud, and there is a time to be quiet and contemplative.

What occupies your mind? What is your ratio of seriousness to silliness? The quality of your thoughts determines whether you are a serious person or silly one. Who will be invited to the court as an adviser, and who will be removed for being the jester?

Trademarks of the Unserious

- **The unserious *never* take responsibility.**
  An unserious person always blames others (including the Devil) for all his or her shortcomings. Things always seem to happen to him or her. God created us to live with intent and purpose, and that is why He gave us free will. We have the right to *choose* how we live—whether good or bad—and we must take responsibility for our choices. However, the unserious person plays the victim and passes the buck. The book of Proverbs describes such a person as a fool.

An American doctor who lived in Africa for twenty-five years was asked what he believed the difference was between witchcraft and medical science. He replied, "When a man gets sick, science asks, '*What* is responsible?' whereas witchcraft asks, '*Who* is responsible?'" A fool will always ask *who* rather than *what*. You ask a fool, "Why did you steal?" He

31

responds, "It was the Devil." You ask, "Why did you commit adultery?" He responds, "It was the Devil." The Devil didn't sleep with someone else's wife; *you* did. Everyone gets tempted, but you choose whether or not to fall for the temptation. Be responsible, look within, confess, and repent. That's how to be serious.

- **The unserious never have a written plan or goal.**
"I will stand my watch and set myself on the rampart, and watch what He will say to me, and what I will answer when I am corrected. Then the Lord answered me and said: 'Write the vision and make it plain on tablets, that he may run who reads it. For the vision is yet for an appointed time; but at the end it will speak, and it will not lie. Though it tarries, wait for it; because it will surely come, it will not tarry.'" (Habakkuk 2:1–3)

This might sting people who believe that they have goals but don't see the need to write them down. God commands that you write them down for your own good. Someone once said, "A piece of paper never forgets." As time passes, details may get hazy, and you risk losing your grip on God's promise if you do not write it down. Articulating your goals well gives speed to your feet. An unserious person is the one without a map or a compass; his or her journey is slow because he or she will always stop to ask for directions. A person without a written goal or plan is one that remains at a level of mediocrity.

- **The unserious live for shortcuts.**

  "Don't look for shortcuts to God. The market is flooded with surefire, easygoing formulas for successful life that can be practiced in your own spare time. Don't fall for that stuff, even though crowds of people do. The way to life-to God is vigorous and requires total attention." (Matthew 7:13–14 *The Message*)

The world has witnessed many get-rich-quick schemes, such as Ponzi and pyramid schemes. Thousands have lost money on these, and many more will lose money because the lure of easy wealth is always tempting. The unserious person craves the path of least resistance. Unfortunately, that path often leads nowhere.

In every good land or profitable venture, there will always be giants to slay. That is simply God's way, and anything contrary to that is not of Him. God showed the Israelites the promised Canaan—a land filled with milk and honey. But that land had one more thing: giants. So they could enjoy the benefits of the lush land, God expected the Israelites to gird up their loins and go after what was theirs. He needed them to learn a valuable lesson: giants fall.

You have heard it said that it is more profitable to work smart than to work hard. Working smart doesn't mean looking for shortcuts or being lazy; it means looking for the best way to maximize your efficiency. It means sharpening the ax so the tree can fall quicker. But you will still have to exert some force to fell the tree; there is no getting around overcoming resistance. Realize that the process of overcoming resistance is a profitable and fulfilling one. From elementary engineering we learn that the resistance of a filament to electricity causes the light bulb to glow. Until you are ready to overcome resistance through mental, physical, and spiritual ability, you will never inherit your promised land.

- **The unserious overlook the "little things."**
In a divorce court, the presiding judge turned to the wife and asked, "Why do you want to divorce your husband?" The woman replied, "He doesn't tell me he loves me." The judge turns to the husband and asked, "Is this true?" The man replied, "Yes, my lord, but on the day I married her, I told her I loved her. I haven't changed my mind since then, so I don't see the point in saying it every day. Those are irrelevant, mundane things."

It's often said that "perfection is not a little thing but little things make for perfection." Little things can make a huge impact. Solomon understood this when he said, "Catch us the little foxes, the little foxes that spoil the vine" (Songs of Solomon 2:15). People look out for the little things. For example, a signature might seem like an insignificant scribble to some, but it certainly isn't small in the business world. It is your identity, your mark of authenticity. By signing you say, "I verify the content of this document." This is why it is ludicrous for a person who claims to be in business to dispatch an unsigned letter. I do not honor unsigned documents, and I know that most businesses do not honor them either.

Thomas Edison once lost a patent because he placed a decimal point in the wrong place. Imagine that. A decimal point is just a dot, but not taking care of that "little thing" cost him his patent. We've heard of people who had surgeries and shortly after died or became critically ill because "little" items were left in their bodies during their surgeries. The major operation was successful, but the cleanup was botched and ended in tragedy.

Once my wife and I hired a lawyer to represent us in a legal matter, but the judge threw out our case. Why? Most of the legal documents our lawyer filed were either incomplete or drafted incorrectly. In the judgment, the judge wrote, "This is an example of a bad draft; the defendant has a case but has engaged the services of the wrong lawyer." We never dealt with that lawyer again, and we certainly didn't recommend his services. The little things will always matter.

Be Thou Serious ...

Finally, know that if you want to prosper like the blessed man described in Psalm 1, you must put away foolish, unserious behavior. Like they say, a fool and his money (or his destiny) are soon parted.

The Fourth Commandment

Thou Shall Have Foolish Friends

The Ostrich and the Eagle

A short story by Chinny Ugoji

A young eagle, still exhilarated by his newly developed flight skills, flew across a field one day and saw a young ostrich relaxing in the shade. "What are you doing sitting there on such a beautiful day?" asked the eagle.

"Just resting," replied the ostrich. "I've been exercising all day, and Mama says I can take a break."

"How far did you fly?"

"I've flown many miles since I learned to fly!" boasted the eagle.

"Oh, I don't fly," the ostrich cheerfully replied, "I run. I get faster every day. Mama says I'm a quick learner."

"You don't fly?" gasped the eagle. "Every bird can fly! What's special about running—anyone can do that! Now flying, that's where the action is! Your mother is just holding you back because she doesn't want you to see the world."

"I don't think so," replied the ostrich, shaking his head thoughtfully. "I have never seen Mama fly before either. I'm an ostrich, you know. Maybe ostriches don't fly."

"Hogwash!" cried the eagle. "You're just a mama's boy! Why if I was as big as you, I'll bet I could fly to the end of the world and back before nighttime!"

Now, the young ostrich did not like being called a mama's boy. He watched as the eagle circled elegantly in the sky and wondered why he couldn't fly. He looked at his wings critically. His plumage was good, and even though his wingspan wasn't as elaborate as the eagle's, he was sure his wings were just as strong. He made up his mind. "How long will it take to teach me?" He called up to the eagle.

"Not long at all!" was the eagle's confident reply. "It's instinctive! My mother carried me high up in the sky and then dropped me. I just flapped my wings very hard and fast, and before I knew it, I was flying! It's really no big deal. Even I could teach you!"

The ostrich was shocked by the eagle's description. Learning to fly sounded dangerous! His running lessons were nowhere as scary. He wished his mother were there to forbid him to go with the eagle. Suddenly he thought of an excuse not to go flying without looking like a coward. "But how do you get me high enough? You certainly aren't strong enough to carry me.

Oh well, at least we tried." The ostrich relaxed, confident that the eagle would go away.

"You're right," said the eagle, eyeing the ostrich critically. "Tell you what. We'll climb up that tall hill over there and then you can jump. It's high enough to give you time to flap your wings and fly."

Cornered, the ostrich followed the eagle to the top of the hill. The ostrich got really nervous when it was time to take the leap. "What if I don't fly and I fall instead?' asked the ostrich, looking worriedly at the rocks below.

"You won't fall. Just flap really hard and fast and you'll do fine."

But ostrich noticed that the eagle didn't sound as confident as he did when they were on level ground, and he stepped away from the edge of the hill. "Fine!" cried the eagle. "I'll wait for you at the bottom of the hill and cushion you if you fall. But I tell you, you won't!"

So the eagle flew to the ground and beckoned the ostrich to jump. The ostrich closed his eyes and jumped, flapping his wings even before he left the ground. He immediately felt himself dropping. "Harder, harder!" cried the eagle. The ostrich closed his eyes and flapped frantically to no avail. He was not flying.

As the eagle realized that the ostrich was fighting a lost battle, he imagined himself crushed under the weight of the large bird and at the last second stepped aside rather than break the fall as promised. The ostrich fell at his feet.

The ostrich, severely wounded but not dead, thanks to the little momentum generated from his rigorous flapping, weakly looked at eagle and asked, "Why didn't you break my fall like you promised?"

The eagle replied, "I'm sorry you couldn't fly, but if I'd caught you, you would have crushed my wings. No point in both of us not flying, is there?"

Weak from his injuries, the ostrich could only look at his ex-mentor incredulously. The eagle shrugged, flapped his wings, and took off, saying, "I'll go get help. You're right: ostriches can't fly. But that's only because they are really slow learners."

He who walks with the wise men will be wise, but the
companion of fools will be destroyed.
—Proverbs 13:20

Who are your best buddies? When you need advice or want to
share some news, what are the first names that come to mind?
Those are the people who directly or indirectly influence the
direction of your life.

In the previous chapter I shared that God has given each of us
free will. While we may not be able to choose our families, we
can all choose our friends. King David handpicked his mighty
men. First Chronicles 11:10 says, "These were the chiefs of
David's mighty men—they, together with all Israel, gave his
kingship strong support to extend it over the whole land, as
the LORD had promised" (NIV).

While our Lord Jesus was here on earth, He also chose His
closest companions. Mark 1 records that as Jesus walked by
the Sea of Galilee, He called James, John, Simon (Peter), and
Andrew. He later chose eight other men to join them. Crowds
followed Jesus throughout his ministry, but He carefully
selected the people that would be closest to him.

If you run a business, you must deliberately choose the people
who will join you at the helm of affairs. You have the right to
let go of a person who chooses to remain foolish despite all
your efforts to the contrary. It doesn't matter if the person
is a sibling—you must distance yourself from foolishness.

Many run their businesses on sentiment, and this is why their business does not prosper. God will not accept the presence of a foolish sibling, family member, or school friend as an excuse for your failure to complete your assignment. Even if you don't want to stir dissension, be wise; send help to those foolish family members but keep them far from your circle of influence. This is not being mean; it is guarding your heart with all diligence. Your life and destiny depends on it (Proverbs 4:23).

Ecclesiastes 10:10 says, "If the ax is dull, and one does not sharpen the edge, then he must use more strength; But wisdom brings success." Wisdom gives you an edge in life, and one way to get wisdom is to garrison your life with wise, godly people. We become the people around us. Two wise people will be wiser, and two silly people will be sillier—that's the way it works.

To remain in the realm of stupidity, you must make and maintain stupid friends. Proverbs 7:17 says, "Iron sharpens iron." People rub off on each other. When you surround yourself with the wrong kind of people, just one evil suggestion can corrupt your heart and jeopardize your future. Do not hang around people of questionable morals or ideals. Learn to identify foolishness from afar, and take off in the opposite direction. For instance, what business does a married man have with a womanizer? It is just a matter of time before you engage in an affair, whether of the body or of the heart.

The Price of Walking with Fools

First Kings 12 gives a sad account of the effect of surrounding yourself with stupid friends. Rehoboam, the son of King Solomon, ascended to the throne after the death of his father. The people approached the new king and appealed to him to lighten the workload Solomon had put on them while he was alive. Rehoboam asked the people to give him time to ponder their request and then sought counsel from the elders of the land. The elders advised that if Rehoboam would show compassion and serve the people by lightening their load, the people would love him and serve him faithfully in return.

However, Rehoboam was dissatisfied with their counsel and turned away to seek counsel from the young men he had grown up with it. These young men told him that it was his time to shine and outdo his father. They advised him to tell the people that they didn't know what a yoke truly felt like, and that in comparison, Rehoboam's finger would be thicker than his father's waist. Rehoboam decided to choose the advice of the youth over that of the elders.

When the people heard, they revolted against his reign and caused Israel to split in two. Rehoboam became ruler over Judah, and Jeroboam became ruler of Israel. For the first time, Israel was ruled by someone outside David's lineage, all because Rehoboam insisted on consorting with fools. Remember, Proverbs 13:20 says, "The companion of fools will be destroyed."

Many people are guilty of acting with the recklessness and stupidity of Rehoboam. Think about it: What qualification did the young men have to advise Rehoboam? Why would anyone elect the counsel of a ruffian over that of a seasoned professional? I believe Rehoboam was a fool long before he ascended the throne, which is why he didn't recognize wise counsel even after he heard it. First Kings 12:8 says, "He consulted the young men who grew up with him." He had kept company with stupid people for far too long, and they jeopardized his destiny.

Checking Your "Fool Meter"

Here is a test that will help you monitor your circle of friends.

1. Get a notepad and write the names of the seven people closest to you. If you are married, your spouse should be the first on your list. If you have children, they should fill the next spot. Just tag it "children." After those first two, add five more names. It's okay if you are not able to list seven people; some people are not as outgoing as others. But you should have between four and five names.

2. Evaluate the names on your list. They are your future. If the people on this list aren't advanced spiritually, physically, and mentally, that spells trouble. If they are progressive people, good for you. You are less likely to be derailed on your way to your destiny.

3. Identify the "stupid" people in your life. These are people who have no moral compass, do not have the fear of God, have no ambition, or fall into the category of the unserious.

4. Cross the names of the stupid people off your list. In so doing, you are crossing them from a place of influence in your life. To do that you must deliberately limit your interactions with them. This is not to say they should become your enemies, but dial your relationship down to the barest minimum.

5. Find new companions. Look for people who have the qualities of the wise. Those are the people you want to get close to and to have rub off on you. This is an important step, because after you cut people from your life, there will be a vacuum. If you do not fill it, you might find yourself going back to the stupid people for companionship.

Remember that the company you keep is and will always be your own choice. There will always be wise people to befriend. Rehoboam could have swapped his foolish young friends for the wise elders, who were more befitting company for a king. Exercise your right *not* to be the companion of fools, and your life will take on a whole new dimension.

The Fifth Commandment

Thou Shall Stick to Thy Guns

Of Mice and Cheese

Excerpts from *Who Moved My Cheese?* by Spencer Johnson, MD

If you do not change, you can become extinct.
Anticipate change.
Be ready to change again and again.
Adapt quickly to change.
Enjoy change.

Smell the Cheese often so you know when it is getting old.
Old beliefs do not lead you to New Cheese.
The quicker you let go of old cheese, the sooner you find New Cheese.
Imagining enjoying New Cheese, even before you find it, leads you to it.
Movement in a new direction helps you find New Cheese.

Ask yourself—"What would I do if I weren't afraid?"
When you move beyond your fear, you feel free.
When you see that you can find and enjoy New Cheese, you change course.
It is safer to search in the maze than remain in a cheeseless situation.
Read the handwriting on the wall: Noticing small changes early helps you adapt to the bigger changes to come.

"Thou shall stick to your guns"—in other words, "Thou shall be pigheaded" or "Thou shall be as stubborn as a mule." Stubbornness is a special division of foolishness; it is required to be a long-term fool. It's only a fool who feels that he or she is too big to change his or her mind.

There is a time to stick to your convictions and a time to bow to superior facts. If we open our hearts to Him, God reveals new information every day that causes us to increase in learning. As we increase in wisdom, some of our preconceived notions are knocked out by superior facts. Superior facts can be garnered via varied means, such as through books, sermons, lectures, or even by observation. These means present the opportunity to change our attitude. A fool is a person who despises superior facts in favor of his or her own weaker, less intelligent position.

Casting Out Your Inner Mule

Are you stubborn and proud of it? Some people now view stubbornness as a virtue and not a vice. It's one thing to be dogged or to display tenacity and grim persistence, but it's another thing entirely to be stubborn. Stubbornness connotes a negative kind of doggedness: an obstinate refusal to change ones attitude or position in spite of good reasons or arguments to do so. Some people just feel they can't be wrong. That is so ridiculous, because no one on this side of heaven is perfect. The foundation for stubbornness is pride or arrogance, and neither of these qualities has a place in the kingdom of God.

Here are some examples of mule foolishness:

- **Refusal to repent:** Some people face the full import of the gospel of Jesus Christ but still insist that they can get to heaven on their own terms. People argue that they are essentially good and believe that they will make heaven based on their good works. The Bible says in John 3:3, "Unless a man be born again, he cannot see the kingdom of God." That is a fact. Works will not get you to heaven; only repentance and being born of water and of the Spirit will.

- **Refusal to forgive:** "I will never forgive that person!" Have you ever heard somebody say that? Many people have been through unspeakable hurt and pain at the hands of others, but while our minds can justify the grudge, our spirits put up a superior argument: to forgive is divine, and to refuse to forgive is to deny the very nature of God in us. Here is another compelling reason to forgive: Matthew 6:14 says, "If you forgive men their trespasses, your heavenly father will also forgive you. But if you do not forgive men their trespasses, neither will your Father forgive your trespasses." It is foolishness to deny yourself God's forgiveness because you want to hold on to a grudge. It doesn't matter what that person did; purpose to forgive him or her so that your walk with God will not be hindered.

- **Refusal to love:** Jesus said, "But love your enemies, do good, and lend, hoping for nothing in return; and your reward will be great, and you will be sons of the Most High" (Luke 6:35). God instructs that we take forgiveness a step further. We are to *love* our enemies. This is how we show that we are children of God. Jesus loved those who persecuted Him, even as He drew His last breath on the cross. Some people believe that loving your enemy or turning the other cheek is a sign of weakness. Others say it will water down their "street cred." That's a weak argument. God's Word is the highest form of credibility anybody needs. Sticking to your guns in the face of that is just foolishness.

- **Refusing to give**: Jesus said, "Give and it will be given unto you, good measure, pressed down, shaken together, and running over will be put into your bosom. For with the same measure that you use, it will be measured back to you" (Luke 6:3). There are people all over the world who argue about giving to the poor, giving offerings to the church, or paying their tithes. They have all sorts of examples about how charities misappropriate funds, how church ministers only want to line their coffers, and how tithing is an "old-school mentality." Yet the Bible, which is our final authority, says that we must give tithes and offerings and that when we give to the poor, we lend to God (Proverbs 19:17). Yet people refuse to obey God's Word and wonder why they don't get blessed or why the devourer seems to attack their finances. Sorry, but you cannot be mule headed about giving and still expect abundance from God. You can't have it both ways: you must serve God or serve yourself.

- **Refusal to learn:** Proverbs 1:5 says, "A wise man will hear and increase learning. And a man of understanding will attain wise counsel." Times have changed and are still changing. At a time when social media is all the rage, some people have refused to learn how to use the Internet and refuse to believe that online transactions are the future of commerce. A refusal to learn relevant skills and update their business practices will soon render them redundant. A refusal to learn new things is foolishness.

- **Refusal to admit wrongdoing:** "I'm sorry." It's such a simple phrase, yet it is so difficult for a mule to articulate. Some married couples will keep malice for weeks because neither party will admit being at fault. They would rather have their prayers hindered than surrender their stubborn pride. Some people never admit to stealing, even when they are caught with their hands in the cookie jar. What manner of folly is that? Second Kings 5 gives the account of the healing of Naaman the leper and the corresponding curse on Gehazi, who was Prophet Elisha's protégé. Naaman had just been healed of leprosy and wanted to give Elisha lavish gifts to show his appreciation, but Elisha refused his gifts and sent Naaman on his way. However, Gehazi couldn't believe that Elisha would allow such bounty to slip through their fingers and went behind his master's back to receive gifts from Naaman. The Lord revealed Gehazi's greed and misdeeds to Elisha; but when he was confronted, Gehazi denied any wrongdoing. As a result of his lies, Elisha cursed Gehazi, and Naaman's leprosy fell on Gehazi and his descendants forever. The interesting thing about this story is that there is no account of Gehazi ever admitting his deceit or repenting of his sin. Perhaps if he had fallen on his face before God, God would have forgiven him and cleansed him. Rather, it seemed Gehazi preferred the disease of leprosy to saying a few simple words: "I was wrong. I'm sorry. Please forgive me."

Stubbornness is truly required for long-term foolishness. There is no pride in being stubborn, pigheaded, or resistant to change. Be quick to repent, slow to discountenance superior facts, and always willing to change directions in favor of the leading of God's Spirit.

The Sixth Commandment

Thou Shall Have a Biased Memory

Ignoring the Signs

The disciples had forgotten to take any food and had only one loaf with them in the boat. Jesus spoke seriously to them, "Keep your eyes open! Be on your guard against the 'yeast' of the Pharisees and the 'yeast' of Herod!"

And this sent them into an earnest consultation among themselves because they had brought no bread. Jesus knew it and said to them,

"Why all this discussion about bringing no bread? Don't you understand or grasp what I say even yet? Are you like the people who 'having eyes, do not see, and having ears, do not hear'? Have your forgotten—when I broke five loaves for five thousand people, how many baskets full of pieces did you pick up?" "Twelve," they replied. "And then there were seven loaves for four thousand people, how many baskets of pieces did you pick up?" "Seven," they said.

"And does that still mean nothing to you?" he said. (Mark 8:14–21 Phillips)

Amnesia is a medical condition where a person experiences a partial or total loss of memory. Some people voluntarily develop another kind of memory loss called *selective amnesia*. Selective amnesia means that one actually chooses or selects memories to discount. Folly requires that a person conveniently forget the things that he or she finds unfavorable or painful. What such a person forgets is that pain itself is an instructor.

For example, suffering a headache is a signal that you are not taking care of your body properly. This should prompt you to examine your habits and ask relevant questions. Is the headache caused by stress, lack of sleep, a poor diet, or emotions? Whatever the cause, pain signals a need for improvement, and when we make the necessary adjustments, the pain eases. If you elect to erase memories of the pain, you end up doing the things that brought the pain on in the first place.

Many people don't learn if they don't experience some pain, and so pain can act as God's megaphone. Sometimes we walk around oblivious of the damage we are doing to ourselves, and it isn't until we experience a tragedy that we realize we have to make a change.

Practicing selective amnesia to forget your pain is a quick way to secure a place in the realm of the foolish. For example, let's say John goes to a club, parties all night, wakes up late in the morning, gets to work not only late but also disoriented and unproductive, and gets a query from his boss. The wise thing for him to do is to learn from the pain of the reprimand and adjust his night crawling activities. But John decides to forget his boss' reprimand and instead remembers the wild time he had at the bar and plans his next escapade. Selecting to forget the reprimand will be detrimental to his performance at work and will ultimately ruin his career. A biased memory can lead you down the path of destruction.

The Power of Memory Preservation

In the bestselling book *The Jewish Phenomenon*, author Steven Silbigier examines the root of the uncommon wisdom and success that is the trademark of the Jewish race. As most of us know, in spite of great persecution and hardship, the Jews have excelled in every field, be it science, arts, or commerce. Silbigier expounded on seven things that he believes are responsible for what he calls as the Jewish Phenomenon; one of those things is the strength of their culture.

My daughter took a course on religious education and was required to study the Jewish festival Hanukah. By the time she was done studying, she knew that Hanukah is an eight-day festival during which the Jews celebrate the Passover and remember when God delivered Israel from the tyranny of Egypt. She learned about the menorah (the lighting of candles) and all the other rites. If she who studied only because it was part of the curriculum knew all these details by heart, imagine how well versed a Jewish child is, who is probably reminded daily of God's mercy to the children of Israel.

The Jewish culture is fiercely preserved and handed down from generation to generation. They still celebrate Hanukah and all the other feasts and traditions God instigated as recorded in the Old Testament. When they entered into the Promised Land, God told the Israelites not to practice selective amnesia. They were not to forget the pain and suffering of the past, because that pain resulted in victory. God was their deliverer. They were to recount these stories to the next generation and keep the memories alive.

Another cultural practice they have preserved came from Exodus 12:17–22: what we now know as the bar mitzvah. When a Jewish boy turns thirteen, his father presents him to the community, saying, "This is my son in whom I am well pleased; you can do business with him. Wherever he stands, he can represent me." A bar mitzvah is the father's way of saying, "When you respect my son, you respect me. When you disrespect him, you disrespect me." It is a legacy of trust and confidence.

Do you know how much esteem this practice gives Jewish children? How many of us craved such words of pride and confidence from our parents when we were growing up? In Africa, the average child must be seen and not heard. He or she should not look an adult in the eye, much less conduct business on a father's behalf. The Jews are so committed to empowering their children that they also created a similar ceremony for their daughters, called a bas mitzvah. Even the girls need to know that they are of a special, chosen, favored people. The Jews have not forgotten a tradition that started in the time of Moses. Rather, they have built on it to make sure they never forget.

The knowledge of their history of triumph over tyranny and God's special favor toward them does something to the psyche of average Jews. They are born knowing that God favors them and that they *cannot* be defeated. They know that they have been tried and tested and that they are a formidable force. They refuse to forget who they are and where they come from.

Remember, Remember, Remember

To celebrate a breakthrough, you must remember the pain you have overcome. If you forget the pain, you forfeit the testimony of the breakthrough. In my seventeen years as a pastor, I have seen people experience a lot of pain. Some of them are convinced that God has forgotten about them—but it is *they* who have forgotten how God delivered them in times past. When I counsel some of these discouraged people, I remind them of the good things God did in the past and encourage them to remember that they have a legacy of victory.

I remember a woman who was discouraged because she lost her job. She was so disheartened that she stopped attending church. When I saw her, I reminded her about the time when she was in the university and a lecturer swore that she wouldn't graduate. God faithfully stepped in, and she graduated. I encouraged her to remember the Lord and His faithfulness. Later this woman got an opportunity to study abroad. Fast-forward a few years to today: she has worked with several multinationals, currently lives abroad, and earns a sizeable income. At the time when she thought God had forgotten, she only needed to remember that God was in the business of delivering His people in grand style.

Always remember God's correction—especially the ones that hurt—because God only chastises the children He loves (Hebrews 12:6). Remembering will give you the grace to plough through any pitfall you may face in the future. If you choose to forget, there will be no reference point for you to believe by faith that God can do much more than He's already done. May your soul *always* bless the Lord. *Never* forget *any* of His benefits.

The Seventh Commandment

Thou Shall Continually Criticize

The Farmer, the Mule, and the Wife

Author unknown

An old country farmer had a wife who constantly nagged him unmercifully. From morning till night she was always complaining about something. The only time he got relief was when he was out plowing the field with his old trusted mule. Hence he tried to plow a lot.

One day, when he was out plowing, his wife brought him lunch in the field. He drove the old mule into the shade, sat down on a stump, and began to eat his lunch. Immediately his wife began nagging him again.

It went on and on.

Suddenly the old mule lashed out with both hind feet, caught her smack in the back of the head, and killed her dead on the spot.

At the funeral several days later, the minister noticed something odd. When a female mourner would approach the old farmer to offer condolences, he would listen for a minute, and then nod in agreement. But when a man mourner approached him, he would listen, and then shake his head in disagreement.

This was so consistent that after the funeral, the minister took him aside and asked him why he nodded his head and agreed with the women, but always shook his head and disagreed with all the men.

The old farmer said, "Well, the women would come up and say something about how nice my wife looked or how pretty her dress was, so I'd nod in agreement."

"And what about the men?" the minister asked.

"They wanted to know if the mule was for sale."

There is a reason that, as blessed as the Jews were, God made them wander in the wilderness for forty years before inheriting the Promised Land; the people delivered from Egypt were masters in the practice of the seventh commandment of foolishness. If there was anything that generation of Israelites was good at, it was complaining and criticizing. They complained about everything: the food, the water, the weather, the laws of God, and even who and how to worship.

The worst part was that their complaints never made sense. It took very little for them to accuse Moses of wrecking their lives by delivering them from slavery. And at the slightest sign of discomfort, they extolled the virtues and the wonders of captivity in Egypt. In Numbers 11, the Jews criticized Moses so much, he became suicidal. God was tempted to wipe the entire race off the face of the earth, but because they were so close to the Promised Land, He spared them.

In Numbers 14, Moses sent twelve spies to the land of Canaan, probably in the hopes that it would excite the people and stir faith and gratitude in their hearts toward the Lord their God. Moses was in for a shock. Ten of the spies returned with reports that though the land was indeed fruitful, giants overran it, and the Israelites were mere grasshoppers in their sight. In other words, God had set them up to be slain by giants, and there was absolutely no way the Promised Land could ever be theirs. In summary: God lied.

The Israelites then declared that they would rather die in the desert or return to slavery than attempt to possess the land that God had given them. That was the final straw. God looked at them and said that, apart from the two spies (Caleb and Joshua) who brought back a good report; they would get their wish: all the Israelites would die in the wilderness.

Today we would call the Israelites whiners. Whiners grate on people's nerves. Have you ever encountered a child who whines? Initially, that child may get what he or she wants, but one day an adult will say, "If you do not stop whining, I will not answer your request." That was the way it was with the Israelites. God had had enough of their childishness. What else could He do for people who were so myopic and who foolishly refused to remember or acknowledge His power?

A Criticism-Free Holiday

There are many present–day "Israelites"—people who cannot go a day without complaining about something. Some people can't go a single day without criticizing their spouse. If you are married, I want to suggest a marriage exercise. Consider one day a week a criticism-free day. Let it be your Sabbath from complaints. Make every effort to see only your spouse's good side, and celebrate him or her throughout that day. And do not store up complaints to read out to him or her the next day. As you go along, increase the frequency of the criticism-free days, and I believe you will get to the point where you are more inclined to support each other than to nag about each other's weaknesses.

Full-time critics aren't only at home though. At work, some supervisors complain about everything. Do you know that sometimes subordinates don't maximize their potential because they are broken down by all the complaints they have to bear? They are so weighed down by the supervisor's yammering that they end up making more mistakes, which only makes the boss criticize them more.

Ken Blanchard, the author of *The One Minute Manager,* encourages managers to commit to one minute of praise. Determine to catch your subordinates doing something right instead of something wrong. Some people see only the tiny errors and discount the massive good.

A person who always whines and criticizes ends up doing far more harm than good. The Israelites complained so much they got to Moses, and he, in an uncharacteristic display of bad temper, disobeyed God. That act of rebellion born of frustration cost Moses the Promised Land. God allowed him to see Canaan, but he was not permitted to dwell in it and died without experiencing the promise. Avoid foolish full-time critics, lest they water down your reasoning and cause you to act as foolishly as they do.

Even Jesus bore the brunt of criticism. In Matthew 11:2, John the Baptist sent his disciples to ask Jesus, "Are you the

Coming One, or do we look for another?" At the time, John was in prison. He probably expected Jesus would do something about it and got offended when Jesus didn't. However, Jesus rose above the thinly veiled accusation and replied in verse 5–6, "The blind see and the lame walk; the lepers are cleansed and the deaf hear; the dead are raised up and the poor have the gospel preached to them. And blessed is he who is not offended because of me."

This is the way we should respond to critics: let your fruit speak for you. If, however, you are on the side of those who constantly criticize, cease from your foolishness. I will end with Paul's admonition to the Colossians: "Be gracious in your speech. The goal is to bring out the best in others in a conversation, not put them down, not cut them out" (Colossians 4:6 *The Message*).

Conclusion: Get Wisdom

If you become wise, you will be the one to benefit. If
you scorn wisdom, you will be the one to suffer.
—Proverbs 9:12 NLT

At the heart of this book is the fact that Wisdom is and always
will be the principal thing (Proverbs 4:7). However, the Bible
isn't referring to just any type of wisdom or to amassing
worldly knowledge that only puffs up. God wants you to
pursue heavenly wisdom. Knowledge is the accumulation of
information, while wisdom is the quality of having experience,
knowledge, and good judgment. Wisdom is the quality of
being wise.

A friend told me long ago that while he was a pharmacy
student in the University, a professor taught them how to
produce aspirin—yet the professor was broke. My friend
asked himself, "If this man knows how to produce aspirin,
why doesn't he get a license and produce enough to sell?"
Knowledge simply amasses information; wisdom applies
it. My friend decided then and there that he would turn his
knowledge to wisdom and make products that he would sell.
Today he runs his own business.

Wisdom is often proven by results. Like we say in my part of the world, "No result, no respect." Even so, sometimes people are so dazzled by results that they fail to look for wisdom. The Bible provides a blueprint for a wise person.

> Who is wise and understanding among you? Let him show by good conduct that his works are done in the meekness of wisdom. But if you have bitter envy and self-seeking in your hearts, do not boast and lie against the truth. This wisdom does not descend from above, but it is earthly, sensual demonic. For where envy and self-seeking exist, confusion and every evil thing are there. But the wisdom that is from above is first pure, then peaceable, gentle, willing to yield, full of mercy and good fruits, without partiality and without hypocrisy. Now the fruit of righteousness is sown by those who make peace. (James 3:13–18)

In Africa, many run after displays of power, not realizing that the balance of power is wisdom. In the frantic search for power, people visit herbalists who claim to have the power to make them rich. Shouldn't wisdom drive you to ask why the herbalist is dirt poor? Can a person give what he or she doesn't even have? Some people even have these illiterate herbalists pray on their pens so that they will pass their exams. A blind clamor for power is foolishness. Study to show yourself approved. (2 Timothy 2:15) You do not need evil shortcuts to succeed in life.

When Jesus was criticized for ministering to and dining with sinners, He said, "Wisdom is justified by our children" (Luke 7:35). A wise person is known by the kind of fruits he or she bears. The fruits of Jesus' ministry were apparent for all to see. God's wisdom is accompanied by His power. The wisdom from above is pure and brings results.

From James 3 we see that wisdom works *in* you before it starts working *for* you. Wisdom alters the way you think, the way you react, the company you keep, your lifestyle, your carriage, and your ministry. It is wisdom not knowledge or a university degree that will help you build an effective home, marriage, business, church, and nation. It is wisdom that will ensure that you fulfill your destiny.

Thank you for reading this book. I believe that you have made the decision to shun foolishness and embrace wisdom. Proverbs 1:7 makes us understand that wisdom starts first by submitting and acknowledging the lordship of God. If you have not surrendered your life to Jesus the Christ, I encourage you to say this simple prayer:

> Lord Jesus, I ask that you forgive me my sins. I acknowledge that I am a sinner and that my sins have separated me from you. I accept the Lord Jesus as my personal Lord and Savior. I ask that you come into my heart and be the Lord of my life. In Jesus' name, amen.

If you have found hope and encouragement from reading this book and would like to receive more information about this book, the author, or this ministry, please contact us.

The Elevation Church
Telephone: +234 700 ELEVATE (700 353 8283)
E-mail: leadpastor@elevationng.org
Website: www.elevationng.org